I0464000

TEN STEPS FOR HOMEBUYERS

MELINDA PAYAN

ISBN: 978-1-4834-7012-2 (sc)
ISBN: 978-1-4834-7013-9 (e)

Library of Congress Control Number: 2017910346

Lulu Publishing Services rev. date: 06/30/2017

To my mother, who is a retired teacher and has always been my inspiration and my hero

"Home is the nicest word there is."

Laura Ingalls Wilder

Contents

Preface

The truth is that there is not much out there to really explain to consumers the basic understandings of going through the mortgage process.

Many of the disclosure packets or HUD counseling centers seem to be filled with confusing literature, without a clear description of the process.

After twenty years in the mortgage industry, I felt that this was a much-needed book. This is an easy-to-read guide about how to protect yourself and what to expect during the mortgage process.

Introduction

This book is designed to help home buyers understand the important points of the mortgage process. It also explains many things one should consider before looking for a home. It is very important that a home buyer have a plan prior to starting the mortgage process. I feel that this book is a great guide to planning one of the most important purchases a person can make.

Monthly Budget

STEP 1

Set a Monthly Budget for a Mortgage Payment

Ask yourself how much you want to spend each month on your mortgage. Make a plan of a set number to not go past. Tell your loan officer to base his or her prequalification of your ability to get a mortgage on this figure. Often, loan officers will try to get you to a higher loan amount or the maximum you qualify for because all loan officers work off a percentage of the loan. The higher the loan, the more money they make.

Stick to your plan!

Notes

Out-of-Pocket Expenses

STEP 2

Figure Out How Much You Want to Pay out of Pocket to Cover All Costs

Ask yourself how much you can afford out of pocket for a down payment and all closing costs. Keep in mind that your down payment is a percentage of your loan, but you also have closing costs and items that are called *prepaid items*. Closing costs are onetime costs associated with getting the loan done. Prepaid items are things you will pay on a regular basis, such as your insurance on your home, which must be prepaid for the first year.

The bottom line is that it is still money coming out of your pocket up front, so make sure you are clear with the loan officer that you want to know what all your expenses will be and not go over whatever number you have established as cash out of your pocket.

Notes

Loan Officer

STEP 3

Research Your Loan Officer

Now that you have a plan, the next step is to find a loan officer who will do an accurate job in prequalifying you. This is really the toughest part because many people do not realize that a loan officer working for a bank does not need to be licensed. His or her only requirement is a background check.

The best place to start is to check your loan officer's qualifications on the National Mortgage Licensing System (NMLS) consumer access website: http://www.nmlsconsumeraccess.org. This website will allow you to see the loan officer's work history, and you can see how many years of experience the loan officer currently has completed.

Notes

Loan Program

STEP 4

Understand Your Loan Program

You must understand the programs your loan officer is suggesting to you. Is your loan officer suggesting an FHA loan as opposed to a Fannie Mae loan? Ask him or her why. Did you know that the FHA requires a down payment of 3.5 percent but Fannie Mae requires a down payment of 3 percent? Many loan officers want to take the easier route with their customers, and that sometimes may be an FHA loan. Make sure you ask questions. Oftentimes, it is more profitable for the lender to offer you an FHA loan as opposed to a Fannie Mae loan, and loan officers tend to not explain why one loan is better than the other.

Notes

Loan Estimate

STEP 5

Get Estimates of the Costs in Writing

Ask your loan officer for an estimate, in writing, of all the costs that he or she is quoting you. Typically, you can avoid paying lender fees, such as underwriting, processing, or loan origination fees, or points by negotiating with the loan officer. Ask the loan officer what he or she is estimating for your annual taxes and annual insurance rates. Check with your real estate agent or a professional in the area to see whether that is consistent with what you should expect. If the taxes or insurance are significantly different, that will drastically affect what you pay each month as well as how much you are qualified for. If you are working with a loan officer who is not local, he or she often makes mistakes that could lead you to not qualifying for the loan later on.

Notes

Other Costs

STEP 6

Find Out about Other Costs

Find out about other fees that the loan officer may not disclose to you. Loan officers are not required to disclose all costs, like inspections. You most likely will want to get a home inspection on your new prospective home. Also, in many states, the insurance companies require additional inspections to make sure the house is up to par. Make sure you ask your loan officer if he or she has included an estimate of those costs. Often loan officers don't include those costs. Speak with a local insurance agent in your area or a local real estate agent, and find out what those costs average.

The last thing you need is to come up with more money unexpectedly.

Notes

Shop Around

STEP 7

Shop Around for the Best Interest Rate and Fees

Shop around! Did you know that you can shop around for many services associated with buying a house? Of course you can shop around for the loan, such as comparing interest rates and fees, but you can also shop around for other associated costs or services. Below is a list of services that you can shop for.

- title work, which is commonly done by an attorney or title company to ensure that you are buying the property free of any liens
- surveying to map the perimeter of your property, which is required for the lender
- homeowner's insurance
- home inspector or inspection company

It is important to note that when you are shopping for interest rates with lenders, do not let more than one lender pull your credit. You do not want to have multiple inquiries on your credit. You can simply tell the loan officer what you believe your credit score is and let him or her give you a quote based on that score before making a decision as to which lender you will choose.

Also, don't let your loan officer tell you that he or she has some special program and you are lucky you qualify, since chances are another company has the same program.

Notes

Gather Documents

STEP 8

Gather Documents

Gather all your documents. Be organized. You will typically need the following just as a starting point:

- last two years of your tax returns (all pages and schedules)
- last two years of your W-2s or 1099s
- last thirty days of pay stubs
- last two months for all bank statements and any other liquid assets you are disclosing, such as retirement accounts or stocks and bonds
- copy of your official ID
- explanation letter for any derogatory credit that is on your credit report, even if it is very old
- gift letter, if you are getting a gift for the down payment (usually a form letter the lender will provide you; other documentation will be required to show where you got the gift from)

Notes

Review Your Income

STEP 9

Make Sure Your Income Was Reviewed Accurately

This is extremely important! Make sure your loan officer has reviewed your tax returns and pay stubs before he or she prequalifies you—not just your W-2s but also your actual returns. Even if you are 100 percent sure your income is simple to figure out, you must be sure this is done.

Many loan officers do not do a thorough job in the beginning, and it can lead to heartache and money loss for you later on. Specifically, ask your loan officers the following questions:

1) Do I have any unreimbursed employee expenses that lower the income that I can use for my loan application?
2) Do I have any Schedule C losses that lower the income I can use for my prequalification?
3) Did I average out my overtime, commissions, or bonuses over a two-year period in order to determine what I qualify for?

I find this is the biggest area where most loan officers make mistakes. They do not check everything up front.

Notes

Interest Rate

STEP 10

Ask about Rate Lock-In Policies and Procedures

Understand the lender's interest rate lock-in policy! When does the loan officer anticipate locking your interest rate in?

Will he or she lock your interest rate in right away? How long will it be locked in for?

Do they offer a "float-down" option if the interest rates improve? If so, is there a cost?

What if you don't close on time to make the lock? What will happen to the locked interest rate?

What will be the cost to extend the interest rate?

Know your rights and your options!

Remember this: know before you owe!

Notes

Conclusion

In conclusion, if you follow these ten steps to guide you through the home-buying process, it will make your experience a lot smoother. You will be more prepared for the road ahead before you start the process.

1) Set a monthly budget for a mortgage payment.
2) Figure out how much you want to pay out of pocket to cover all costs.
3) Research your loan officer.
4) Understand your loan program.
5) Get estimates of the costs in writing.
6) Find out about other costs.
7) Shop around for the best interest rate and fees.
8) Gather documents.
9) Make sure your income was reviewed accurately.
10) Ask about interest rate lock-in policies and procedures.

Glossary

appraisal: A report that the lender orders to determine the value and condition of the property.

APR: The annual rate earned by a borrower, expressed as a percentage. This is not what your loan payment is based on. This is a percentage that takes into account any costs you have paid for the loan too.

debt-to-income ratio: The amount of your debt compared to your gross monthly income. Every loan has a certain debt-to-income ratio you cannot exceed.

escrow account: When you pay your taxes and insurance with your mortgage payment, this account is required. When you first close on your loan, the lender requires a certain number of months of reserves to be placed in an account with the lender's financial institution. Then every month, the lender puts a prorated portion of your payment that applies toward taxes and insurance into that account. The institution pays the taxes and the insurance from this account as well. If you ever sold the house or paid off the loan, this money would be refunded to you.

escrow deposit: This is the deposit that is required to be made per the terms of the contract. This amount is negotiated with the terms of your offer.

lender's title insurance: This is an insurance policy that insures the lender there will be no other liens on title before the lender's lien position. This is required with all mortgages.

loan commitment: Generally, all loan commitments are what are called conditional loan commitments. This means that the loan is approved based on the borrower providing certain loan conditions.

loan to value: This is a percentage that compares the loan to the value of the property. For example, if you are putting down 20 percent on a property, the loan to value is 80 percent.

lock in: This term refers to whether your interest rate is locked in. If your interest rate is not locked in, your rate can go up.

owner's title insurance: This is an insurance policy that insures the new owner that there will be no other liens on title that will affect his or her ownership. A good example of this is when a prior owner had work done on the house and the tradesman comes back years later claiming he was owed money and tries to file a mechanic's lien. In this situation, the owner's title insurance would protect the new owner.

prequalification or preapproval letter: A letter that is usually asked for prior to shopping for houses. This means that you have applied for a mortgage and have passed the initial requirements to be considered prequalified.

prepaid items: These are costs that you must pay at closing that are prepaying things in advance. For example, the first year of homeowner's insurance must be paid one year in advance.

Schedule C: The tax schedule where someone who is either self-employed or receives a 1099 reports his or her income.

Schedule E: The tax schedule where someone who is either self-employed and owns a corporation or receives rental income reports his or her income.

survey: A map of the perimeter of the property. This is important because it lets the buyer and the lender know whether there are any encroachments. For example, a neighbor may have a fence on the property line of the house you are buying. This also will tell you whether there are any easements that utility companies have deemed that you cannot build on.

unreimbursed employee expenses: These are expenses that a person who is not self-employed may be able to deduct on his or her tax returns. An example of this is a nurse can deduct the cost of her uniforms. The reason why this is important is because, depending on the loan you apply for, the lender may have to deduct the expenses from your income. This would cause you have less income and possibly qualify for less of a home.

The Truth About Lending LLC is a licensed mortgage company. NMLS #1054357

12401 Orange Drive Suite 207, Davie, Florida 33326

The material in this book is not an offer for extension of credit nor a commitment to lend. Programs, rates, terms and conditions subject to change without notice. Certain restrictions may apply. All approvals subject to underwriting guidelines. Not all applicants will qualify.

The Truth About Lending
can be reached at

888-76-TRUTH or at
www.thetruthaboutlending.com

Like us on Facebook at
https://www.facebook.com/
TheTruthAboutLending

follow us on Twitter at @truthaboutlend

12401 Orange Drive Suite 207
Davie, Florida 33330

About the Author

Melinda Payan has more than twenty years of experience as a licensed investment broker, licensed mortgage broker, and licensed Realtor. She has been president of the Truth About Lending since 2010. Prior to that, she was the president of Rose Financial Group for more than ten years. Melinda was also the host of *The Truth About Lending* radio show, where consumer advocacy always came first.

Because of her extensive training and knowledge in the field of mortgages, she is able to offer clients and the general public an expert look at the mortgage industry today.

Melinda values providing a personalized approach to assist people in making the best mortgage choices. Combining a professional and caring style, she has been able to expand her success in the industry into a mission and a passion to reach out and educate the general public and put the truth back into lending!

Notes

Notes

Notes

Notes

Notes

www.ingramcontent.com/pod-product-compliance
Lightning Source LLC
Chambersburg PA
CBHW021932170526
45157CB00005B/2289

* 9 7 8 1 4 8 3 4 7 0 1 2 2 *